JNF 940.53 DOE 2009
Doeden, Matt
Weapons of World War II

DATE DUE

6	9	

WEAPONS OF WAR

WEAPONS OF
WORLD WAR II

by Matt Doeden

Reading Consultant:
Barbara J. Fox
Reading Specialist
North Carolina State University

Content Consultant:
Tim Solie
Adjunct Professor of History
Minnesota State University, Mankato

Capstone
press®

Mankato, Minnesota

Blazers is published by Capstone Press,
151 Good Counsel Drive, P.O. Box 669, Mankato, Minnesota 56002.
www.capstonepress.com

Library of Congress Cataloging-in-Publication Data
Doeden, Matt.
    Weapons of World War II / by Matt Doeden.
    p. cm. — (Blazers. Weapons of war)
    Includes bibliographical references and index.
    ISBN-13: 978-1-4296-1972-1 (hardcover)
    ISBN-10: 1-4296-1972-4 (hardcover)
    1. Military weapons — History — 20th century — Juvenile literature.
2. World War, 1939–1945 — Equipment and supplies — Juvenile literature.
I. Title. II. Series.
UF500.D685 2009
623.409'044 — dc22   2008000525

Summary: Describes the weapons of World War II, including small arms, larger
weapons, and vehicles.

Editorial Credits
Mandy Robbins, editor; Alison Thiele, set designer;
    Kyle Grenz, production designer; Jo Miller, photo researcher

Photo Credits
AP Images, 12, 25, 27, 29 (aircraft carrier); BigStockPhoto.com/JJ23, 28 (M3
scout car); Corbis, 26; Corel, 8–9, 10, 13 (Colt .45 pistol, Mauser Karabiner 98k,
P38 pistols); Dreamstime/Tiono, 21 (Flak 88 mm field gun); Getty Images Inc./
American Stock, 24; Getty Images Inc./Central Press, 29 (U-boat); Getty Images Inc./
Hulton Archive, cover (bottom right), 15, 20 (Fat Man bomb); Getty Images Inc./
Keystone, 7; Getty Images Inc./LAPI/Roger Viollet, 23; Getty Images Inc./MPI, 20
(Little Boy bomb); Getty Images Inc./Time Life Pictures/David E. Scherman, 16;
Getty Images Inc./Time Life Pictures/George Strock, 18; Getty Images Inc./Time Life
Pictures/Ralph Morse, 9; Getty Images Inc./Time Life Pictures/William C. Shrout,
29 (PT boat); The Granger Collection, New York, 5; The Image Works/Scherl/
SV-Bilderdienst/Lessman, 11; iStockphoto/Ian Ilott, 20 (coastal gun); iStockphoto/
Nancy Nehring, 28 (B-17 bomber); iStockphoto/sgame, 13 (M34 machine gun);
iStockphoto/Tom De Bruyne, 21 (field gun, bottom); James P. Rowan, 20 (railway
gun), 21 (210 mm field gun), 28 (M5 tank), 29 (USS *Alabama* battleship, USS *Cassin
Young* destroyer); ©Jupiterimages Corporation, cover (bottom left), 13 (grenades);
NARA, 19; Shutterstock/Dwight Smith, cover (top), 28 (P-40 fighter plane);
Shutterstock/EchoArt, 13 (MP40 machine gun); Shutterstock/Marilyn Volan (grunge

TABLE OF CONTENTS

A BLOODY WAR

Soldiers storm an enemy beach during a World War II (1939–1945) battle. Explosions rock the ground. Gunfire echoes.

WEAPON FACT

Germany invaded Poland on September 1, 1939. This event marked the start of World War II.

WWII battle re-creation

World War II was a huge war. The **Axis powers** fought against the **Allies**. From pistols to bombs, World War II weapons caused big damage.

Allies — countries including England, France, and the United States that fought together in World War II

Axis powers — countries including Germany, Italy, and Japan that fought together in World War II

WEAPON FACT

The United States entered the war in 1941 after Japan bombed Pearl Harbor, a U.S. Naval base in Hawaii.

GUNS AND GRENADES

The most popular weapon of World War II was the rifle. Germans carried the Mauser Karabiner 98k. U.S. soldiers fired M1 Carbine rifles.

Mauser Karabiner 98k

U.S. soldier with rifle

Colt .45 pistol

Pistols worked well in close fighting. The Colt .45 was lightweight and easy to handle.

WEAPON FACT

Many World War II soldiers flung explosives called grenades at enemies.

German hand grenade

M2 machine gun

The German MP40 was a small but powerful **machine gun**. The U.S. M2 was an even more powerful machine gun.

machine gun — a gun that fires bullets quickly without needing to be reloaded

SMALL ARMS

U.S. Colt .45 pistol

German P38 pistols

Mauser Karabiner 98k rifle

German MP40 machine gun

German M34 machine gun

grenades

BIGGER WEAPONS

Bazookas shot small rockets.
Soldiers used them to blow up
enemy vehicles. A bazooka
blasted through 5 inches
(12.7 centimeters) of metal.

bazooka

105 mm howitzer

Field guns chattered across battlefields. Germans fired Flak field guns. U.S. soldiers shot howitzers.

field gun — a large, powerful gun that is sometimes called an artillery gun

WEAPON FACT

U.S. soldiers gave the howitzer the nickname "Arty," which was short for artillery.

The Germans mounted huge guns to railway cars. These guns shot 7-ton (6.4-metric ton) shells. In 1945, the United States dropped two `atomic bombs` on Japan. The bombs were named Fat Man and Little Boy.

`atomic bomb` — a bomb that destroys large areas and leaves behind harmful elements called radiation

14-inch railway gun

WEAPON FACT

The atomic bombs that fell on
Japan killed between 80,000
and 140,000 people.

LARGE WEAPONS

Little Boy atomic bomb

Fat Man atomic bomb

German coastal gun

German 280 mm
railway gun

German Flak 88 mm field gun

German 210 mm field gun

field gun

DEADLY VEHICLES

Deadly vehicles roamed
World War II battlefields.
Tanks had huge guns and
strong armor.

armor — metal covering that
protects military vehicles

German Panzer tank

23

Warplanes filled the sky. Japanese Zeroes battled U.S. P-51 Mustangs. Bombers attacked from high above the action.

U.S. P-51 Mustang

U.S. aircraft carrier

Battleships, aircraft carriers, and
destroyers fought on the sea. Submarines
cruised underwater. They shot enemy
ships on the ocean's surface.

For six years, World War II raged on the Pacific Ocean and in Europe. The war's powerful weapons left a lasting mark on the world.

WEAPON FACT

U.S. Navy sailors on Patrol Torpedo (PT) boats used torpedoes to sink much larger warships.

U.S. Navy PT boat

VEHICLES

U.S. M5 light tank

U.S. M3 armored scout car

U.S. B-17 bomber

U.S. P-40 fighter plane

U.S. aircraft carrier

German U-boat

U.S. Navy PT boat

USS *Alabama* battleship

USS *Cassin Young* destroyer

GLOSSARY

Allies (AL-lyz) — a group of countries including the United States, England, and France that fought together in World War II

armor (AR-muhr) — a heavy metal layer on a military vehicle that protects against bullets or bombs

atomic bomb (uh-TAH-mik BOM) — a powerful explosive that destroys large areas; atomic bombs leave behind harmful elements called radiation.

Axis powers (AK-siss POW-uhrs) — a group of countries including Germany, Japan, and Italy that fought together in World War II

field gun (FEELD GUHN) — a large, powerful gun; field guns are also called artillery guns.

machine gun (muh-SHEEN GUHN) — a gun that can fire bullets quickly without needing to be reloaded

torpedo (tor-PEE-doh) — an explosive weapon that travels underwater

READ MORE

Black, Hermann. *World War II.* Wars Day by Day. Redding, Conn.: Brown Bear Books, 2009.

Harris, Nathaniel. *World War II.* Timelines. North Mankato, Minn.: Arcturus, 2007.

Herbst, Judith. *The History of Weapons.* Major Inventions through History. Minneapolis: Twenty-First Century Books, 2006.

INTERNET SITES

FactHound offers a safe, fun way to find Internet sites related to this book. All of the sites on FactHound have been researched by our staff.

Here's how:

1. Visit *www.facthound.com*
2. Choose your grade level.
3. Type in this book ID **1429619724** for age-appropriate sites. You may also browse subjects by clicking on letters, or by clicking on pictures and words.
4. Click on the **Fetch It** button.

FactHound will fetch the best sites for you!

INDEX